PRESIDENTIAL (Mis)SPEAK
The Very Curious Language of George W. Bush™
Volume 2

Edited by

Robert S. Brown

★ ★ ★ ★

 **Outland Books**
Outland Communications, LLC
Skaneatclcs, New York

For information about discount purchases or purchasing Outland's George W. Bush
Desk Calendars, please contact Outland Books at (315) 685-8723 or www.outlandbooks.com

Published by Outland Books
Outland Communications, LLC
P.O. Box 534
25 Hannum Street
Skaneateles, New York 13152

www.outlandbooks.com

ISBN: 0-9714102-4-0

Design by HumanDesign

Printed in the United States of America

To my wife, Joni, for her ongoing encouragement and to my children for their true appreciation of this project.

"I try to go for longer runs, but it's tough around here at the White House on the outdoor track. It's sad that I can't run longer. It's one of the saddest things about the presidency."

George W. Bush

"And so, in my State of the—my State of the Union— or State—my speech to the nation, whatever you want to call it, speech to the nation—I asked Americans to give 4,000 years—4,000 hours— over the next—the rest of your life—of service to America. That's what I asked—4,000 hours."

George W. Bush

INTRODUCTION

I have a story to tell... My family resides in a quaint picturesque village nestled on the northern end of one of New York's Finger Lakes. One might describe our small and peaceful town as having been painted by Norman Rockwell - a perfect little slice of Americana. A throwback to the 1950s. No McDonalds or Wal-Marts here in our carefully crafted community.

Every year in early summer as the tourist season reaches its zenith, our village's downtown merchants host a three-day sidewalk sale. Capitalizing on the stunning beauty of Central New York's gently rolling hills and long slender lakes, our town's retail district becomes a festival of tents and balloons with every kind of craft and knick-knack for sale. Crowds swarm the brick-trimmed sidewalks. Children with ice cream cones and popcorn are everywhere. Two tranquil parks provide repose for those wishing to gaze out at the relaxing scene of sailboats gliding their way across the sparkling waters of our deep, cold, glacially-carved lake.

So, I thought, how ideal. A wonderful opportunity for my girls to make some spending money and learn a little something about commerce. Therefore, Outland Books became a paying member of the Chamber of Commerce and the Downtown Merchant's Association, rented a table and tent and my three high school-aged children set about selling the Presidential (Mis)Speak series of books and calendars.

Well, my girls learned a lesson but it had nothing to do with commerce. They were given a short and intensive course on intolerance. In their first morning of work they were treated to roughly 10 verbal tongue lashings by adult passersby. They were accused of being "Unpatriotic". They were told they "Didn't Love Their Country", that they were too young to be "Politicking" on the street, that it was "Shameful" what they were doing. Finally one women, with raised voice, demanded they close down and take their anti-American demonstration home. Calmly my 18 year-old offered that this wasn't any kind of demonstration, that the content of our material was humor, and that the women had the choice of just walking on.

The women walked on, right to the president of the Chamber of Commerce and insisted we be expelled. When this request was denied she called the police and demanded we be forcibly removed. Dutifully, in order to determine the circumstances of the situation, the police responded and this is when I was called at my office. My wife was the caller and she was understandably distraught that our children were being subjected to such hostility.

For the next two and a half days my wife and I took turns sitting with our girls under our rented tent. Curiously, with adults present the verbal attacks ceased for the most part. There was one man who asked me if I was aware that the president was a religious man. After answering in the affirmative I was told that such a man of God shouldn't be ridiculed in this sort of disgraceful way.

Thankfully, the experience wasn't all discouraging. After our skirmishes were reported by the local media, a few shoppers commended our little band of subversives for persevering and keeping our chins up. Good for those few people. They give us all hope.

RSB

"All Americans...
need to watch what they say, watch what they do."

Ari Fleischer
White House Press Secretary
Washington, D.C.
September 26, 2001

PRESIDENTIAL SPEAK

"Do you have blacks, too?"

November 8, 2001   Comment made to Brazilian President Fernando Henrique Cardoso during a White House meeting in Washington, D.C. As reported by Fernando Pedreira on April 28, 2002, in *Estado Sao Pauloan* and subsequently reported in the German publication, *Der Spiegel*, May 19, 2002.

"Behind these statistics are great personal achievements. Adversity had been overcome and lives have changed forever. I've met people all around our country who can share their stories of hard work and fighting odds that have been stacked against them. Moms and dads who are battled addiction."

January 14, 2003   Speaking on the topic of welfare reform.

PRESIDENTIAL SPEAK

"Border relations between Canada and Mexico have never been better."

September 24, 2001   Joint press conference with Canada's Prime Minister.

★ ★ ★ ★

Reporter: "Mr. President, is Secretary Powell going to provide the undeniable proof of Iraq's guilt that so many critics are calling for?"
Bush: "Well, all due in modesty, I thought I did a pretty good job myself of making it clear that he's not disarming."

January 31, 2003   Press conference with British Prime Minister Tony Blair at the White House.

★ ★ ★ ★

"The law I sign today directs new funds and new focus to the task of collecting vital intelligence on terrorist threats and on weapons of mass production."

November 27, 2002 Speaking at the White House during the signing of the September 11th Commission Bill.

★ ★ ★ ★

"Perhaps the biggest problem is that we have passed children from grade to grade, year after year, and those child haven't learned the basics of reading and math."

January 8, 2003 Speaking at the White House about the "No Child Left Behind Act".

★ ★ ★ ★

PRESIDENTIAL SPEAK

"This country has no designs on Cuba's soverty; we have no designs on the soverty of Cuba."

May 20, 2002   Remark at Cuban Independence Day event at the James L. Knight Center in Miami, Florida.

"Matter of fact, there haven't been a morning that haven't gone by that I haven't saw—seen—or read threats…"

November 12, 2002   Remarks by the President at the District of Columbia Metropolitan Police Operations Center, Washington, D.C.

"Clear Skies legislation, when passed by Congress, will significantly reduce smog and mercury admissions, as well as stop acid rain."

April 22, 2002   Calling for conservation and stewardship. Whiteface Mountain Lodge in Wilmington, New York.

The Very Curious Language of George W. Bush™
Volume 2

PRESIDENTIAL SPEAK

"When a fellow American has more money in his or her pocket they're more likely to demand a good or a service. And in the marketplace which we have in America, when somebody demands a good or a service, somebody is more likely willing to produce that good or a service, and when somebody produces the good or a service it means somebody is more likely to find work."

January 29, 2003   Speaking in Grand Rapids, Michigan.

★ ★ ★ ★

"When we focus on the greater good, we can get a lot done… So I want to congratulate the members of both political parties on this anniversary for working so hard to accomplish a significant and meaningful piece of legislation. And, now, we gotta get to work. Now we gotta do the job that's expectus."

January 8, 2003 Speaking before a group in the White House about the "No Child Left Behind Act".

"They will not hold America blackmail."

September 5, 2002 Referring to America's terrorist enemies during a speech in Indiana.

PRESIDENTIAL SPEAK

"These measures will help our economy grow and that's important for the federal budget. It's important for state budgets. If you're worried about budgets, which we should be worried about budgets, the first question you ask is how do we create growth in the economy?"

January 29, 2003   Grand Rapids, Michigan.

"You've got to have certainty in the system that requires risk."

November 7, 2002   Discussing making tax cuts permanent at a press conference outlining the President's priorities.

PRESIDENTIAL SPEAK

"Parents and educators will not be bystandards in education reform."

January 8, 2003   Speaking before a gathering in the White House on the "No Child Left Behind Act".

★ ★ ★ ★

"I'm using this as an opportunity to make a point on judicial reform. And that is that if a judge thinks he's going to retire, give us a year's notice, if possible. And then we will act. We, the administrative branch, will nominate somebody and clear them within 180 days."

November 7, 2002   The President speaking from the White House and referring to the 'Executive Branch' of the U.S. Government, over which he presides.

★ ★ ★ ★

PRESIDENTIAL SPEAK

"We must understand that the consequences we take to make the area more secure also, uh, must be in—these decisions to make the area more secure must be made in the context of peace for the long run."

August 1, 2002   Speaking at the White House during a joint press conference with King Abdullah of Jordan.

★ ★ ★ ★

"These are the far most reaching reforms of American business since Franklin Roosevelt was the President."

December 10, 2002   During the swearing-in ceremony of the Securities and Exchange Commission's new director, William Donaldson.

★ ★ ★ ★

The Very Curious Language of George W. Bush™
Volume 2

PRESIDENTIAL SPEAK

"If Russia thought that the neighborhood was unsettled, it might create some issues. But Poland has provided a great source of stability in the neighborhood, and therefore Russia feels less threatened. And I think that's an important nuance, as we say in foreign policy. I think that's the word, isn't it? Nuance?"

July 17, 2002 White House press conference with the Polish President.

"One year ago today the time for excuse-making has come to an end."

January 8, 2003 Speaking at the White House on the one-year anniversary of the signing of the "No Child Left Behind Act".

PRESIDENTIAL SPEAK

"We expect Saddam Hussein, for the sake of peace, to disarm. That's the question."

January 14, 2003   Speaking to the press in the Oval Office during a visit from Polish President Aleksander Kwasniewski.

"In order for there to be peace in the Middle East, we must route out terror wherever it exists. And the U.S. effort to route out terror around the world is going to benefit the Middle East in the long term."

January 28, 2002   Addressing the press while meeting with Hamid Karzai, the Afghan Interim Government Chairman.

"With us, as well, is two other fine members of the congressional delegation from Pennsylvania."

January 16, 2003 Making introductions during a speech at the University of Scranton in Pennsylvania.

Bush: "I want to thank and welcome Geno Auriumma. Is that right?"
Mr. Auriemma: "Auriemma."
Bush: "Auriemma. Okay, fine. I've never been too good in English. But, he's a heck of a coach, however he says his name."

May 21, 2002 White House introduction of Geno Auriemma, the head coach of the NCAA Championship University of Connecticut women's basketball team.

Indian Reporter: "First of all, my apologies for not having the tie, because I have this Indian summer suit today."

Bush: "Oh, that's OK—therefore you don't get to ask a question."

[laughter]

[The question was then asked and answered]

Bush: "If you had worn a tie you could of had a follow-up [question]."

July 8, 2002   White House press conference.

"I understand taking tests aren't fun."

January 8, 2002   Addressing students at Hamilton High School in Hamilton, Ohio.

Bush: "James is a installation supervisor. He is eh, ah, he is a tax-payer. He is a man who's got a daughter that he cares a lot about… The tax plan speaks to people like James Thomas. Welcome."

J. Thomas: [Speaks for 14 seconds.]

Bush: "You got more to say than that."

February 13, 2003   Jacksonville, Florida.

"There's inspectors in the country now."

December 5, 2002   Referring to Iraq. Speaking from the White House.

"This administration will route out terror wherever it exists, and will hold people accountable if they harbor a terrorist, or made up a terrorist, or threaten the United States with terrorist weapons."

February 27, 2002 Speaking at a fund raising event for United States Senate candidate Elizabeth Dole in Charlotte, North Carolina.

"Today we got Pamela Hedrick with us today."

January 14, 2003 Introducing a former welfare recipient at a White House function.

PRESIDENTIAL SPEAK

"We're here for have a substanative talk on a lot of issues."

January 14, 2003   Speaking in the Oval Office about his meetings with the visiting Polish President Aleksander Kwasniewski.

★ ★ ★ ★

"We'll work with Speaker Hastert, Leader Delay and Congressman Pelosi, as well."

January 6, 2003   CongressMAN Nancy Pelosi is the Democratic leader of the House of Representatives, the first woman to hold that position.

★ ★ ★ ★

"We're working on what's called 10-plus-10-over-10… to help Russia securitize the dismantling—the dismantled nucular warheads."

May 23, 2002   Remarks while meeting with German Chancellor Schroeder in Berlin, Germany.

The Very Curious Language of George W. Bush™
Volume 2

"First of all, I appreciate the wisdom of Chairman Greenspan. He uses the word, 'soft spot'. I use the word, 'bumpin along'."

November 13, 2002 Answering a question regarding the state of the economy after meeting with the Cabinet in the White House.

★ ★ ★ ★

"The goals for this country are peace in the world. And the goals for this country are a compassionate American for every single citizen."

December 19, 2002 Speaking at a Washington, D.C., food bank.

★ ★ ★ ★

PRESIDENTIALSPEAK

"These are folks that have hijacked a great religion and then take innocent life. And that's a huge difference between America."

September 27, 2002   Speaking in Denver, Colorado.

★ ★ ★ ★

"I can tell you how good of folks they are, not only in terms of the jobs they'll have, but just in the quality of character."

December 18, 2000   Speaking to the press and referring to his cabinet appointees.

★ ★ ★ ★

PRESIDENTIAL SPEAK

"Policies that stimulate growth ought to be the centerplace of public policy."

January 29, 2003   Grand Rapids, Michigan.

"Robin Hayes—he needs to go back to Washington, D.C. He needs to be reelected for the good of North Carolina workers and North Carolina business owners… He's one of the best grass roots politicians I've ever met… He also sted strong for the textile industry."

February 27, 2002   Speaking in Charlotte, North Carolina, at a fund raising event for Elizabeth Dole, candidate for the United States Senate. The President is referring to United States Congressman, Robin Hayes, who is running for reelection.

PRESIDENTIAL SPEAK

"Tommy (General Tommy Franks) knows the lessons of Vietnam just as well as I do… He graduated from high school in '63 and you and I graduated in '64. We're of the same vintage. We paid attention to what was goin' on. And ah, and so ah,—I think it was '64, wasn't it?"

March 13, 2002   Speaking to a reporter at a White House press conference.

"Let me reinerate what I just said, this is a matter of weeks, not months."

January 31, 2003 Referring to U.S. demands that Iraq reveal its weapons of mass destruction.

The Very Curious Language of George W. Bush™
Volume 2

PRESIDENTIAL SPEAK

Bush: "Zimbabwe… we are dealing with—and we are dealing with our friends to figure out how to deal with this flawed election."

Reporter: "What are the options then?"

Bush: "Well we're dealing with our friends right now to figure out how to deal with it."

March 13, 2002 White House press conference.

"We look forward to today that no child in this country is ever left behind."

January 8, 2003 Speaking on education reform at a White House ceremony.

PRESIDENTIAL SPEAK

Reporter: "The accounting procedures at Harkin and Aloha have been compared to what went on at Enron. Would you agree with that?"

Bush: "No."

Reporter: "Why not sir?"

Bush: "There was no **mál**feeance involved. This was a honest disagreement about accounting procedures… There was no **mál**feeance; no attempt to hide anything."

July 8, 2002   (bold with accent mark = accented syllable) The President had business dealings with Harkin and Aloha energy companies prior to entering politics. White House press conference.

★ ★ ★ ★

PRESIDENTIAL SPEAK

"And so, in my State of the—my State of the Union—or State—my speech to the nation, whatever you want to call it, speech to the nation—I asked Americans to give 4,000 years—4,000 hours—over the next—the rest of your life—of service to America. That's what I asked—4,000 hours."

April 9, 2002   Speaking in Bridgeport, Connecticut.

"I've not made up our mind about military action."

March 6, 2003   White House press conference. Washington, D.C.

PRESIDENTIAL SPEAK

"And most importantly, Alma Powell, secretary of Colin Powell, is with us."

January 30, 2003 The President is referring to Secretary of State Colin Powell's wife, Alma.

"I can report to the American people that these five soldiers, badly injured in the line of service, are gettin' the best possible care."

January 17, 2003 Speaking at the Walter Reed Army Medical Center in Washington, D.C.

"If you don't have any ambitions, the minimum wage job isn't going to get you to where you want to get."

August 29, 2002 Speaking in Little Rock, Arkansas.

The Very Curious Language of George W. Bush™
Volume 2

PRESIDENTIAL SPEAK

Barbara Walters: "Isn't it all—so much of it—about oil? Shouldn't we be changing our energy policy?"
Bush: "The war on terror has nothing to do about oil."

December 13, 2002 Speaking to Barbara Walters of ABC News during a White House interview.

"The welfare laws is a success because it puts government on the side of personal responsibility."

January 14, 2003 Addressing the issue of welfare reform.

PRESIDENTIAL SPEAK

"There is no question we have obligations around the world... there's a major obligation there (in South Korea) of 37,000 troops, an obligation that is an important obligation, one that I know is important and we will keep that obligation."

March 13, 2002 White House press conference.

★ ★ ★ ★

"Jackson from Texas, you got anything of Texas question?"

November 7, 2002 Offering a reporter the opportunity to ask a question during a White House press conference.

★ ★ ★ ★

PRESIDENTIAL SPEAK

"Sometimes I get a little wordy, I admit that."

December 19, 2002 Comment from a speech at a Washington, D.C., food bank.

"We should not be satisfied with the current numbers of minorities on American's college campuses."

January 15, 2003 Speaking at the White House on the issue of affirmative action as it applies to college entrance policies.

"One of the reasons why prices is rising is because of frivolous and junk lawsuits against our medical community."

October 22, 2002 Speaking on medical malpractice in Downingtown, Pennsylvania.

PRESIDENTIAL SPEAK

"We had some of our fellow citizens think they could fudge the books and we're routin' 'em out and bringing them to justice."

January 29, 2003   Speaking in Grand Rapids, Michigan. Referring to recent corporate scandals.

"Elaine Chow... she's the Secretary of the Department of Labor. When we're interested in jobs, we think about the Department of Labor."

January 14, 2003   Speaking on the topic of welfare reform at the White House.

"My interest is to reduce the threat of a nucular war, is to reduce the number of nucular warheads… If need be, we'll just reduce unilaterally to a level commiserate with keeping a deterrence and keeping the peace."

March 13, 2002   White House press conference.

"There's going to be some hurdles to cross."

September 23, 2002   Speaking in Trenton, New Jersey.

"I understand politics and I know there's gonna be a lot of verbage."

January 2, 2003   Referring to the 2004 campaign for the presidency. Speaking to the press at his ranch in Crawford, Texas.

★ ★ ★ ★

"You've stood with us against a deadly threat. And we will stand with you, to help bring an end to the terrible regional conflicts that brings so much suffering to innocent Africans—from Congro, to Sudan, to the Ivory Coast."

January 15, 2003   Speaking, via video, to the delegates of the second U.S.- sub-Saharan African Trade and Economic Forum.

★ ★ ★ ★

PRESIDENTIAL SPEAK

"Saddam Hussein... must disarm, and that's why I have constantly said and the Prime Minister have constantly said this issue will come to a head in a matter of weeks not months."

January 31, 2003 Speaking to the press at the White House during a visit from British Prime Minister Tony Blair.

"We're not gonna spend money on curriculum that will not teach our children how to read."

January 8, 2003 Speaking at the White House about education reform.

PRESIDENTIAL SPEAK

"And… it's gettin' worse. That's what people have gotta understand up there in Washington, or over there in Washington, down there in Washington, wherever—thought I was in Crawford for a minute."

January 16, 2003 Referring to increases in the cost of medical malpractice insurance. Speaking in Scranton, Pennsylvania (north and slightly east of Washington, D.C.).

"As a society, we must demand something better, because there is no second-rate children in America."

September 5, 2002 Speaking in South Bend, Indiana.

"If you're interested in being a part of feeding those who hunger, this is a great place to come to."

December 19, 2002   Speaking at a Washington, D.C., food bank.

"There was a good news story in Mississippi. I went down there—it wasn't because of me—it was because of the doctors and the citizens understand the cost of a trial system gone array."

January 16, 2003   Speaking on medical liability at the University of Scranton in Pennsylvania.

PRESENTIAL SPEAK

"I know full well that Bin Laden and his cronies would like to harm America again. Bin Laden and his cronies would like to harm our allies. How do I know that? I receive intelligence reports on a daily basis that um, that um, that indicates that that's his desires."

December 28, 2001   Speaking at a press conference in Crawford, Texas.

"I like it here a lot, I really do… We really like it."

August 25, 2001   Referring to his ranch in Crawford, Texas.

PRESIDENTIALSPEAK

"There is some statistics out today that showed our economy continues to grow."

July 31, 2002 Speaking from the White House. Washington, D.C.

★ ★ ★ ★

"I appreciate Lieutenant Governor Judy Kell for being here. Great to see you again Judy."

April 9, 2002 Welcoming Connecticut's Lieutenant Governor, Jodi Rell. Bridgeport, Connecticut.

★ ★ ★ ★

"I like the idea of serious people walking in and saying, 'Mr. President, here are your options; decide.' "

August 10, 2001 Being interviewed by an ABC News correspondent. Crawford, Texas.

PRESIDENTIAL SPEAK

"All of us owe a tremendous debt to this man's towering intellect and his devotion to liberty. So, it's my honor to welcome you all to the White House. Thank you for coming—I'm lookin' forward to havin' lunch."

May 9, 2002   Honoring economist Milton Friedman and his wife, Rose, during ceremonies at the White House.

★ ★ ★ ★

"I was wondering if anybody's got any extra Pepsodent? Get it?"

July 19, 2001   From official "10 Downing St." transcript of a press conference with President Bush and British Prime Minister Tony Blair. A reference to President Bush's comment at a previous meeting with Prime Minister Blair that they both used Colgate toothpaste.

★ ★ ★ ★

PRESIDENTIAL SPEAK

"... while one of us can't do everything to help heal the hurt of America, each of us can do something to help make somebody's life in your community a better place."

January 16, 2003 Speaking in Scranton, Pennsylvania.

"I'm beginning to travel around the country to important states—all states are important, of course..."

February 22, 2001 White House press conference.

PRESIDENTIAL SPEAK

"In order to avoid litigation... docs and therefore the companies that insure them just settle... instead of maybe suffering the consequences of a lousy jury and a lousy verdict."

January 16, 2003   Speaking on medical liability in Scranton, Pennsylvania.

"There's a lot of hot debate that have already taken place."

February 22, 2001   Referring to Congress and his tax relief package. White House press conference.

"John Thune has got a common sense vision for good forest policy. I look forward to working with him in the United Nations Senate to preserve these national heritages."

October 31, 2002   Speaking at Northern State University in Aberdeen, South Dakota.

"I think Mr. Greenspan—not to put words in his mouth—well, why don't I just put some words in his mouth."

February 22, 2001   Referring to Federal Reserve Chairman Alan Greenspan. White House press conference.

PRESIDENTIAL SPEAK

"And so we're putting a full review on the programs."

March 29, 2001 The President is speaking of reviewing the various aid packages extended to Russia by the United States. White House press conference.

★ ★ ★ ★

"The American people are impatient —very patient—and for that I'm grateful."

January 5, 2002 Referring to the reaction of Americans to the war on terrorism. Town hall meeting in Ontario, California.

★ ★ ★ ★

"I appreciate Tommy (Thompson)… I appreciate Elaine Chow… I appreciate Bob Woodson… I appreciate Rodney Carrow… I appreciate John (Gregor)."

January 14, 2003 The President, welcoming members of the audience at a White House function on welfare reform.

The Very Curious Language of George W. Bush™
Volume 2

PRESIDENTIAL SPEAK

"I also want Congress to provide 17 billion dollars a year to help the states run their welfare programs and 4.8 billions a year to help pay for child care."

January 14, 2003   Speaking on welfare reform.

"This is the 15th Cabinet meeting we've had since we were sworn in. I appreciate each of your working so hard on behalf of the American people."

January 6, 2003   Speaking to the press after meeting with his Cabinet in the White House.

"America has stockpiled enough vaccine and is now prepared to inoculate our entire population in the event of a smallpox attacks."

December 13, 2002

"Inherent in a free country is the capacity for killers to come and hide out. But we're in alert. We fully understand the stakes."

December 13, 2002

PRESIDENTIAL SPEAK

"My mom often used to say, 'The trouble with W'—although she didn't put that to words."

April 3, 2002   White House. Washington, D.C.

"Listen, out of the evil done to this great land is going to come incredible good, because we're the greatest nation on the face of the earth, full of the most fine and compassioned and decent citizens."

August 15, 2002   Mt. Rushmore, South Dakota.

"I talked to Cecil from... Columbus, Maryland... his wife said, 'You keep talkin' about the need for mentors but you haven't done a darn thing about it.' Cecil and I married well. Same thing happens to me, Cecil."

January 30, 2003 Speaking at the Boys and Girls Club of Greater Washington on the first anniversary of the USA Freedom Corps.

"We've got another candidate on stage who we certainly hope she wins."

October 22, 2002 Welcoming Melissa Brown, candidate for the United States House of Representatives. Downingtown, Pennsylvania.

PRESIDENTIAL SPEAK

"There was certainly a very strong sentiment that we're on the right track when it comes to holding people to account who lie, steat, or cheal—lie, cheat, or steal—who defraud people by cooking the books."

August 16, 2002   Referring to the President's Economic Forum. Crawford, Texas.

★ ★ ★ ★

"It seems like the more T.V. channels there are, the more anxious people become on T.V."

January 5, 2002   Referring to reaction in the United States to the war in Afghanistan. Town hall meeting in Ontario, California.

★ ★ ★ ★

PRESIDENTIAL SPEAK

"And if Iraq regimes continues to defy us and the world, we will move deliberately, yet decisively, to hold Iraq to account."

September 16, 2002 Davenport, Iowa.

"Prior to September the 11th, we were discussing smart sanctions. We were trying to fashion a sanction regime that would make it more likely to be able to contain somebody like Saddam Hussein."

January 31, 2003 Speaking to the press at the White House during a visit from British Prime Minister Tony Blair.

PRESIDENTIAL SPEAK

"We need action and we need reasonable action without causing a pleth**ór**a of lawsuits."

March 13, 2002 (bold with accent mark = accented syllable) Referring to the need for corporate CEOs to be responsible for their companies' financial statements—in the wake of the Enron scandal. White House press conference.

★ ★ ★ ★

"Here in the midst of all our plenty there are… people who, when you hear the word, 'American Dream', have no idea what you're talkin' about."

December 19, 2002 Speaking at a food bank in Washington, D.C.

★ ★ ★ ★

"This is a part of the world where killing have been going on for a long, long time."

April 18, 2002 Speaking in the Oval Office about the situation in the Middle East.

PRESIDENTIAL SPEAK

"… and when somebody produces the good or service it means somebody is more likely to find work. That's why tax relief is such an important component about creating the environment for economic growth."

January 29, 2003   Speaking in Michigan the day after the State of the Union Address.

"I do believe Ariel Sharon is a man of peace… He is embraced the notion of two states living side by side."

April 18, 2002   Speaking about the Israeli Prime Minister after Secretary of State Colin Powell's trip to the region.

The Very Curious Language of George W. Bush™
Volume 2

PRESIDENTIAL SPEAK

"I absolutely believe that America is gonna make some right choices in life."

February 27, 2002   Speaking in Charlotte, North Carolina, at a fund raising event for United States Senate candidate, Elizabeth Dole.

"Reach into your wallet so that those of us who hurt among us have a chance to heal and to be a part of the American experience. Those who are poor, those who are suffer, those who have less hope are not strangers in our midst."

December 19, 2002   Speaking at a Washington, D.C., food bank.

The Very Curious Language of George W. Bush™
Volume 2

"If everybody receive a vaccine, there are some to whom that vaccine might be fatal."

July 8, 2002 Responding to a reporter's question on who should be vaccinated for smallpox. White House press conference.

"The welfare law of 1996 has enabled millions of Americans to build better lives—better lives for themselves, better lives for their families, and, hence, better lives for our country."

January 14, 2003 Addressing the issue of welfare reform at a White House function.

PRESIDENTIAL SPEAK

"The folks who conducted to act on our country on September 11 made a big mistake… They misunderestimated the fact that we love a neighbor in need. They misunderestimated the compassion of our country. I think they misunderestimated the will and determination of the Commander-in-Chief, too."

September 26, 2001 Speaking at CIA headquarters in Langley, Virginia.

"It's white."

July 19, 2001 The President's answer, when asked by a child in London to describe the White House.

PRESIDENTIAL SPEAK

"The system is less about justice and more about somethin' that looks like the lottery… And with the plaintiff's bar gettin' as much as 40% of any verdict, sometimes there's only one winner in the lottery."

January 16, 2003   Referring to current medical liability laws. Scranton, Pennsylvania.

"I condemn it in the most strongest of terms."

March 27, 2002   Referring to a suicide bombing having taken place during Passover in Netanya, Israel.

PRESIDENTIAL SPEAK

"The American people appreciate Ireland's work… to help secure passage of Resolution 1441… We appreciate our own support for ensuring that the just demands of the world are enforced."

March 13, 2003 Referring to the United Nations resolution requiring Iraq to disarm itself of weapons of mass destruction.

"The reason to create this Department is not to create the size of government but to increase its focus and effectiveness."

June 6, 2002 Speaking from the White House on the need to form a cabinet-level Department of Homeland Security.

PRESIDENTIAL MISSPEAK

"There are people that hide in caves, they hide in kind of the dark corners of society, and they use suiciders as their forward army."

December 13, 2002   Speaking with Barbara Walters of ABC News.

"… nucular… nucular… nucular… nucular… nucular… nucular… nucular… nucular… nucular… nucular… nucular… nucular…"

January 28, 2003   State of the Union Address to the joint session of Congress.

"By preparing at home and pursuing enemies abroad, we're adding to the security of our nation. In fact, the members of my team who are here who are adding to the security of our nation."

December 13, 2002   Announcing a plan to better protect the American people against the threat of a smallpox attack.

★ ★ ★ ★

"I'll reinerate. I have been disappointed in Chairman Arafat."

May 7, 2002   Speaking in the Oval Office with Israeli Prime Minister Ariel Sharon. Referring to Palestinian Chairman Yasser Arafat.

★ ★ ★ ★

PRESIDENTIAL SPEAK

"One of the things we did before comin' over is we had a round-table discussion sitting around a square table."

February 12, 2003   Speaking to a group of "small investors" in Virginia.

"We want people coming to our country that wants to take advantage—you know—that wants to either visit this great country or study in this great country or see relatives in this great country."

January 2, 2003   Speaking to reporters in Crawford, Texas.

PRESIDENTIAL SPEAK

"When I say I'm a patient man, I mean I'm a patient man."

August 21, 2002   Referring to his handling of the Iraq crisis.

Interviewer: "So, do you ever think about Al Gore?"
Bush: "Why? What do you mean?"
Interviewer: "Do you ever wonder what he's up to and think about last Fall?"
Bush: "Not really."

August 10, 2001   Being interviewed by an ABC News correspondent at his ranch in Crawford, Texas.

PRESIDENTIAL SPEAK

"We didn't need any more theory in Washington. We needed people that actually done."

September 17, 2002 Speaking in Nashville, Tennessee, about Secretary of Education Rod Paige.

Interviewer: "Do you ever forget you're President when you come here, when you're just in the canyon by yourself—does it, does that evaporate?"

Bush: "Yeah, kinda—not really."

August 10, 2001 The President being interviewed by an ABC News correspondent at his ranch in Crawford, Texas.

PRESIDENTIAL SPEAK

"Hydrogen power will dramatically reduce greenhouse gas admissions."

February 6, 2003 Speaking on the topic of energy independence in Washington, D.C.

"It was a year ago that I signed the 'No Child Left Behind Education Act'. It was the most meaningful education reform probably ever… This is a, this was a, this was a art of what is possible in Washington."

January 8, 2003 Speaking at the White House about the "No Child Left Behind Act".

PRESIDENTIAL SPEAK

"Congressmen and Senators and their staffs can pick and choose the [health] plan that meets them best."

January 16, 2003   Speaking in Scranton, Pennsylvania, on medical liability.

"But the problem I want to talk today is the problem with our health care system."

January 16, 2003   Speaking at the University of Scranton in Pennsylvania.

"Listen, I understand water. I grew up in Midland, Texas. You remember how much water we didn't have there."

January 5, 2002   Town Hall Meeting in Ontario, California.

"I'm thankful that he's coming across the—actually, coming down from Canada, but coming across the sea to visit us."

February 22, 2001   Referring to British Prime Minister Tony Blair's impending visit to Washington, D.C. White House press conference.

"I've decided to send Secretary of State Powell to the region next week to seek broad international support for the vision I've outlaid today."

April 4, 2002   Speaking at the White House about the gathering crisis in the Middle East between Israel and the Palestinians.

PRESIDENTIAL SPEAK

"In my attitude, it doesn't matter how high the hurdle is, we'll cross it."

February 9, 2003 Addressing members of Congress at a weekend retreat in White Sulpher Springs, West Virginia.

"We have totally routed out one of the most repressive governments in the history of mankind, the Taliban."

January 30, 2002 Speaking in Winston-Salem, North Carolina.

"Cars that will run on hydrogen fuel produce only water, not exhausts fumes."

February 6, 2003 Speaking on energy independence.

The Very Curious Language of George W. Bush™
Volume 2

PRESIDENTIALSPEAK

"Not only are we strong militarily, but we've got great hearts and great compassion about our fellow human men and women."

April 8, 2002   Promoting volunteerism in America. From a speech delivered in Knoxville, Tennessee.

★ ★ ★ ★

"If you're like me, you won't remember everything you did here. That can be a good thing."

May 21, 2001   Addressing students at Yale University, the President's alma mater.

★ ★ ★ ★

PRESIDENTIAL MISSPEAK

"Let me remind you that—and the people who are listening—that accounting in Washington is a little different than the way normal—I shouldn't say normal people—the average person accounts."

February 22, 2001 White House press conference.

"For years, the freedom of our people were really never in doubt."

February 14, 2003 Speaking at FBI headquarters.

PRESIDENTIAL SPEAK

"I've got a lot on my agenda and a lot on my platter."

January 2, 2003   Speaking to the press at the President's Crawford, Texas, ranch.

"We take the continuity of government issue very seriously… and I still take the threats that we receive from Al Qaeda killers and terrorists very seriously… We take every threat seriously… This is serious business and we take it serious-ly."

Circa March 1, 2002   Explaining why the administration had formed a "shadow government" operating in secret somewhere outside of Washington, D.C. Source: Comedy Central's *Daily Show with Jon Stewart*.

PRESIDENTIAL SPEAK

"I love the story that came out of Michigan about the women of cover—of Muslim faith—who didn't feel comfortable about going to their home and so Jewish and Christian groups, ladies' groups, went to the neighborhood and said, 'We'll walk you to the store.'"

January 5, 2002 Speaking of the difficulties suffered by Muslims in the aftermath of September 11, 2001. Town hall meeting in Ontario, California.

★ ★ ★ ★

"Our government has no information that a smallpox attacks is imminent."

December 13, 2002 Press conference about the possibility of a smallpox attack against the United States.

★ ★ ★ ★

PRESIDENTIAL SPEAK

"I want to reinerate what I said the other day. Our policy is to deny sanctuary to terrorists any place in the world, and we will be very actively in doing that."

March 13, 2002   White House press conference.

★ ★ ★ ★

"And we're too close. Our relationship is too strong to endure some of the slights that come along."

January 23, 2002   Referring to his marriage in an interview with Tom Browkaw of NBC News.

★ ★ ★ ★

"Far be it from the American President to get to decide who leads what country."

April 5, 2002 Interview with ITN in Crawford, Texas.

★ ★ ★ ★

"Neighbors in the region... must make it clear that people who suicide bomb are not martyrs—that they kill and murders of innocent people."

April 18, 2002 Referring to nations in the Middle East. During a meeting with Secretary of State Colin Powell after the Secretary's return from Israel.

★ ★ ★ ★

"The federal government and the state government must not fear programs who change lives, but must welcome those faith-based programs for the embetterment of mankind."

August 23, 2002 Stockton, California.

"She had a relative named Eisenhower, and he and I share something in common. We're both Presidents."

October 25, 2001 Referring to Dwight David Eisenhower, the 34th President of the United States and deceased since 1969. Washington, D.C.

PRESIDENTIAL SPEAK

"When I picked somebody to be the Secretary of Education, I didn't want some theorists, I wanted somebody that had actually been in the trenches."

April 24, 2002 Referring to Secretary of Education Rod Paige at a White House ceremony honoring the 2002 National Teacher of the Year.

"Some say, 'give it to the taxpayers who pay the bills.' That some is George W. Bush."

January 22, 2000 Referring to a federal tax rebate. Remark from a speech in Sioux City, Iowa.

PRESIDENTIAL SPEAK

"One of the problems we have is that enough people can't find work in America."

November 4, 2002 Speaking in Bentonville, Arkansas.

"Over 50% of our energy comes from overseas. Fortunately, a lot of it comes from Canada."

January 5, 2002 Remark from a town hall meeting in Ontario, California.

"I want to thank Roy Blunt for bein' a good vote counter and we're countin' on ya to count."

February 9, 2003 Referring to Congressman Roy Blunt. Speaking at a Congressional retreat at the Greenbriar resort in West Virginia.

"The operative question is; 'How soon will you start working on reforms?' If I could put a question in your own mouth. The answer is, 'as soon as possible.' That's what we discussed about."

May 7, 2002 Answering a reporter's question in the Oval Office during a meeting with Israeli Prime Minister Ariel Sharon.

"I'm convinced that the stronger our personal bond is, the more likely it is relations between our country will be strong."

April 25, 2002 Comment made after meeting with Saudi Crown Prince Abdullah in Crawford, Texas.

"... so that an entrepreneur such as yourself are able to learn from other entrepreneurs..."

May 25, 2002   Answering questions at St. Petersburg University in Russia.

"The House has acted on the pension reforms I proposed in February and on the corporate responsibility proposals I made in March. It's time for the Senate to act in a eekaly responsive manner."

July 8, 2002   White House press conference.

"Greg Przybylski was here—the brain doctor."

January 16, 2003   Referring to a prominent neurosurgeon during a discussion on medical liability in Scranton, Pennsylvania.

★ ★ ★ ★

"All of us need to step back and try to figure out how to make the U.N. work better as we head into the 21st century… in the post-Saddam Iraq, the U.N. will definitely need to have a role. And that way it can begin to get its legs—legs of responsibility— back."

March 16, 2003   Speaking at a summit held in the Azores just prior to the beginning of the Iraq war.

★ ★ ★ ★

PRESIDENTIAL SPEAK

"I appreciate so very much the Prime Minister, Jean Chretien, for joining us here. He has been a steadfast friend. I really enjoy dealing with him on a personal basis. He's a plain-spoken fellow with a good sense of humor. Probably won't go too good up here in Canada, but he'd be a great Texan."

September 9, 2002   Speaking in Detroit, Michigan, USA.

"She was neat."

July 18, 2001   Referring to Queen Elizabeth II. Quoted in the *Times* of London.

PRESIDENTIAL⚡SPEAK

Reporter: "Does your goal of catching Osama bin Laden dead or alive, does that still stand?"

Bush: "Yeah—I don't know if he is dead or alive for starters... He may be alive. If he is we'll get 'em. If he's not alive, we got 'em."

July 8, 2002 White House press conference.

"A week ago Yasser Arafat was boarded up in his building in Ramalla... He's now free to show leadership, to lead the world."

May 2, 2002 Comment made during a press conference held with leaders of the European Union in Washington, D.C. Referring to the fact that the Palestinian Chairman, who had been prevented by Israeli armed forces from leaving his compound, was now free to move about.

The Very Curious Language of George W. Bush™
Volume 2

PRESIDENTIAL SPEAK

"Laura loves children a lot, and I'm really proud to call her wife, and she's doing a fine job as our First Lady, and I'm proud of the job she's doing."

July 23, 2003

"Mitch Pearlstein and his wife, Diane, live in Minneapolis. They couldn't be with us today, but I want to share with you his, his, their quick story—their story in a quick way."

July 23, 2002   White House event announcing new adoption initiative.

PRESIDENTIAL SPEAK

"There are some concern about over-stating a numbers."

February 20, 2003 Referring to the improper way in which some corporations determine their profits. Cobb County, Georgia.

Reporter: "Mr. Bush, when can we hope that Jackson-Vanik will be rescinded, which currently is very out of place?"

Bush: "I couldn't make myself clearer during my opening statement about how I feel about Jackson-Vanik."

May 24, 2002 Remarks made at the signing of a nuclear arms treaty with Russian President Vladimir Putin at the Kremlin in Moscow. Jackson-Vanik is an amendment to a 1974 trade act which pertains to trade relations between the U.S. and Russia.

PRESIDENTIAL SPEAK

"They didn't think we were a nation that could conceivably sacrifice for something greater than ourself; that we were soft, that we were so self-absorbed and so materialistic that we wouldn't defend anything we believed in. My—were they wrong! They just were reading the wrong magazine or watching the wrong Springer show."

March 12, 2001   Washington, D.C.

★ ★ ★ ★

"I hope the Congress will extend the unemployment benefits for—for the American workers who don't have a job."

January 6, 2003   Speaking from Washington, D.C.

PRESIDENTIALSPEAK

"It's a war that requires us to be on an international manhunt—we're on the hunt. It's a war that causes us to need to get the enemy on the run— we got 'em on the run."

February 14, 2003   Speaking in Washington, D.C., at FBI headquarters.

★ ★ ★ ★

"I want to thank all my citizens for coming."

October 31, 2002   Speaking in Aberdeen, South Dakota.

★ ★ ★ ★

"I've seen mentor and mentoree and heard their testimony."

January 30, 2003   Washington, D.C.

★ ★ ★ ★

"Well, I agree with Zell, with his economic theory—that when a person has more money in their pocket, they're likely to demand somebody to produce them a good, or a service."

February 20, 2003   In Kennesaw, Georgia, discussing the economy with a group of small business owners.

★ ★ ★ ★

PRESIDENTIAL SPEAK

"Many of the punditry—of course not you, but other punditry—were quick to say no one is going to follow the United States of America."

January 21, 2003 Speaking to the press at the White House. Referring to the United States position on Iraq.

"It is important… that the workers in their countries are not prone to need to work in the narcotics industry."

April 4, 2002 Calling on the Senate to pass the Trade Promotion Authority. State Department, Washington, D.C.

PRESIDENTIAL SPEAK

"The NATO Summit that convenes tomorrow will be the first ever held at the capital of a Warsaw Pact."

November 20, 2002 Comment by the President to the Prague Atlantic Student Summit. Prague, Czech Republic.

★ ★ ★ ★

"I know something about being a government, and you've got a good one."

November 4, 2002 The President is referring to Arkansas Governor Mike Huckabee. Speaking in Bentonville, Arkansas.

★ ★ ★ ★

"When Iraq is liberated, you will be treated, tried and persecuted as a war criminal."

January 22, 2003 Referring to Saddam Hussein. Washington, D.C.

The Very Curious Language of George W. Bush™
Volume 2

PRESIDENTIAL SPEAK

"I'm so pleased that the President and Prime Minister have agreed to come and have a subsantive visit."

December 5, 2002 Meeting with President Moi of Kenya and Prime Minister Meles of Ethiopia in the Cabinet Room of the White House.

"I believe Saddam Hussein is a threat to the American people. I believe he's a threat to the neighborhood in which he lives. And I've got a good evidence to believe that."

March 6, 2003 Speaking at a White House press conference.

PRESIDENTIAL SPEAK

"It is wonderful to be here at Harrison High. I'm honored to be in the presence of the principal, Donny Griggers. I want to thank he and his staff."

February 20, 2003   Speaking in Cobb County, Georgia.

"I want to thank Wolfowitz and Armitage, who are up here with us—two of the prettiest members of my administration."

February 14, 2003   Referring to Paul Wolfowitz and Richard Armitage, Deputy Secretary of Defense and Deputy Secretary of State, respectively (each man very much settled into middle age). Speaking at FBI headquarters.

PRESIDENTIAL SPEAK

"Slowly but surely we're dismantling the Al Qaeda network, and that inures to the benefit of all countries of the world."

December 5, 2002   President Bush meeting with President Moi of Kenya and Prime Minister Meles of Ethiopia at the White House.

"This agency has... ordered corporations and executives to return to investors hundreds of million dollars in improper gains."

February 18, 2003   Referring to the SEC (Securities and Exchange Commission) at a White House event.

PRESIDENTIAL SPEAK

"As we work to keep the peace we've also got to work to make America a better place for all of us. I mean every single citizen. That means we've got to have an education system that is next to none."

September 27, 2002   Denver, Colorado.

"You must know that I am serious— so are a lot of other countries— serious about holding the man to account."

November 7, 2002   White House press conference.

PRESIDENTIAL SPEAK

"Years of habit, years of infrastructure, must be replaced by modern way."

February 6, 2003   Referring to a potential shift to hydrogen as a fuel source for the automobile.

★ ★ ★ ★

"I think the American people—I hope the American—I don't think, let me—I hope the American people trust me."

December 18, 2002   Washington, D.C.

★ ★ ★ ★

"Any Americans who wants to work, can't find a job, we will be committed to job growth."

February 13, 2003   Speaking in Jacksonville, Florida.

"I ran on a political philosophy. I'm not changing my political philosophy. I am who I am prior to—the same guy after the election, prior to the election. That's just who I am and how I intend to lead this country."

November 7, 2002   Press conference at the White House. Washington, D.C.

★ ★ ★ ★

"John Snow is excelled as a business leader."

December 9, 2002   Nomination of John Snow as new Secretary of the Treasury.

★ ★ ★ ★

PRESIDENTIAL SPEAK

"This administration is committed to your effort. And with the support of Congress we will continue to work to provide the resources school need to fund the era of reform."

January 8, 2003 Speaking to secondary school administrators at the White House.

"I may decide to let you a follow-up or not, depending upon—[laughter]— whether I like my answer."

November 7, 2002 At a press conference outlining the President's priorities, in response to a request for a follow-up question. White House.

PRESIDENTIAL SPEAK

"[The space shuttle] Columbia carried in its payroll, classroom experiments from some of our—ah—students in America."

February 3, 2003   Bethesda, Maryland.

"If you're interested in the Kings expanding their business, which I am… They've gots to got to upgrade their equipment."

February 20, 2003   Referring to small business owners during a speech in Cobb County, Georgia.

PRESIDENTIAL SPEAK

"There are a lot of good people workin' on that goal. We've got good people here at the federal level working on it. No better advocate than excellence in public schools than Laura."

January 8, 2003 Referring to his wife while speaking about education reform at the White House.

★ ★ ★ ★

"Cecil… brought his young mentoree with him today. I decided I'd trick the guy and say: 'You got any goals?' "

January 30, 2003 Speaking at a Boys and Girls Club in Washington, D.C.

★ ★ ★ ★

PRESIDENTIAL SPEAK

"Leaders in the region speak of a new Arab charter that champions internal reform, greater politics participation, economic openness, and free trade. And from Morocco to Bahrain and beyond, nations are taking genuine steps toward politics reform."

February 26, 2003 Washington, D.C.

"If this situation persists and judicial vacancies go unfulfilled..."

November 2, 2002 Radio address to the nation.

PRESIDENTIAL SPEAK

"Imagine a system where docs can't share information amongst each other, much less talk to your patient for fear that what they say will be used 'em in court one day."

January 16, 2003 Addressing a crowd in Scranton, Pennsylvania. Discussing medical liability reform.

"This is a chance for the Security Council to show its relevance. And I believe the Security Council will show its revalence—relevance."

February 22, 2003 Joint press conference in Crawford, Texas, with Spanish President José Maria Aznar.

"I don't want to be so discriminatory that people will say that I haven't thought this through."

November 7, 2002   Choosing reporters for questions at a White House press conference.

★ ★ ★ ★

"Washington, D.C., hurt as a result of the attacks of September the 11th. The economy suffered around here; therefore there are more who are hunger and there are less who are giving."

December 19, 2002   Speaking at a Washington, D.C., food bank.

★ ★ ★ ★

PRESIDENTIAL SPEAK

"More and more people are owning small business. That's incredibly important, because that phenomenon makes sure that the elites don't control the economy."

May 25, 2002   Answering questions at St. Petersburg University in Russia.

"I promise you I will listen to what has been said here, even though I wasn't here."

August 13, 2002   President's Economic Forum. Waco, Texas.

PRESIDENTIAL SPEAK

"Over 75% of white Americans own their home, and less than 50% of Hispanics and African Americans don't own their home. And that's a gap, that's a home-ownership gap. And we've got to do something about it."

July 1, 2002 Speaking in Cleveland, Ohio.

★ ★ ★ ★

"We need an energy bill that encourages consumption."

September 23, 2002 Speaking in Trenton, New Jersey.

★ ★ ★ ★

PRESIDENTIAL SPEAK

"The only way to be sure every child is learning is to test regularly and to show everybody, especially the parents, the results of the tests. The law further requires that the test results be presented in a clear and meaningful way so that we can find the learning problems within each group of students. I'll show off a little. It's called *'Disagragation of Results'* (laughter)."

January 8, 2003   Poking a bit of fun at himself during a White House address on education reform.

PRESIDENTIAL SPEAK

"Mr. President… you have distingershed yourself by your service to your country."

December 5, 2002 Meeting with President Moi of Kenya at the White House.

"I was the guy that said they ought to vote. And one country voted—at least showed their cards, I believe. It's an old Texas expression, 'show your cards', when you're playing poker."

March 16, 2003 The President is referring to the United Nations vote on Iraq. He is also referring to a common expression known far and wide outside of the state of Texas.

PRESIDENTIAL SPEAK

"Our government must work to make college more 'fordable for students who come from economically disadvantaged homes."

January 15, 2003 Speaking on the issue of affirmative action and how it relates to college admission policies.

"A new kind of war has now placed our police, firefighters, and rescue workers on the front lines. You're already on the front lines. Now you've got another line."

November 12, 2002 Remarks by the President at the District of Columbia Metropolitan Police Operations Center, Washington, D.C.

PRESIDENTIAL SPEAK

"Our nation will work hard to achieve a peace. He also carried a message that people must be focused and must work hard to achieve a peace."

April 18, 2002   Referring to Secretary of State Colin Powell and his recent trip to the Middle East.

"Today I met with a lot of great health givers and healers—decent people, compassionate Americans who love their patients."

January 16, 2003   In Scranton, Pennsylvania, speaking on the topic of medical liability.

PRESIDENTIAL SPEAK

"The suicide bombings have increased. There's too many of them."

August 15, 2001 Albuquerque, New Mexico.

"The public education system in America is one of the most important foundations of our democracy. After all, it is where children from all over America learn to be responsible citizens, and learn to have the skills necessary to take advantage of our fantastic opportunistic society."

May 1, 2002

PRESIDENTIAL SPEAK

"I try to go for longer runs, but it's tough around here at the White House on the outdoor track. It's sad that I can't run longer. It's one of the saddest things about the presidency."

August 21, 2002   Washington, D.C.

"Most people in Arkansas know where Texas is, and all the people in Texas know where Arkansas is."

March 1, 2001   Speaking to schoolchildren in Little Rock, Arkansas—some of whom, apparently, don't know where Texas is.

The Very Curious Language of George W. Bush™
Volume 2

PRESIDENTIAL SPEAK

"This is an American issue—a uniquely American issue... I say, 'uniquely American issue' because I truly believe that now that the war has changed, now that we're a battlefield, this man poses a much graver threat than anybody could have possibly imagined. Other countries, of course, bear the same risk."

September 26, 2002   Referring to the threat of terrorism. Houston, Texas.

"This foreign policy stuff is a little frustrating."

April 23, 2002   As reported by the *New York Daily News* and the *Guardian*.

The Very Curious Language of George W. Bush™
Volume 2

PRESIDENTIAL SPEAK

"It's hard for me to explain why we need to make [tax cuts] permanent. It's kind of some of the things that happen in Washington. On the one hand, they taketh away. On the other hand, they giveth."

September 27, 2002 Speaking in Denver, Colorado.

"The thing I admire about this Prime Minister is he doesn't need a poll or a focus group to convince him the difference between right and wrong."

April 6, 2002 Remarks at a press conference with British Prime Minister Tony Blair in Crawford, Texas.

"We've got pockets of persistent poverty in our society, which I refuse to declare defeat."

March 18, 2002 O'Fallon, Missouri.

The Very Curious Language of George W. Bush™
Volume 2

PRESIDENTIAL SPEAK

"I know that we have got the technologies necessary to explore in a places like Alaska without damaging the environment."

January 5, 2002 Referring to oil exploration. Town hall meeting in Ontario, California.

★ ★ ★ ★

"The budget I submitted holds growth... to 4%. That's about as much as the average America's family's income is expected to grow this year."

February 20, 2003 Speaking in Cobb County, Georgia.

★ ★ ★ ★

"I'm going to work with every Cabinet member to set a series of goals for each Cabinet."

January 2, 2001   News conference to name cabinet nominees. Austin, Texas.

"Millions of—thousands of people— millions of dollars and thousands of people—millions of dollars aren't being invested and thousands of people aren't working."

November 1, 2002   Addressing a crowd in Portsmouth, New Hampshire.

The Very Curious Language of George W. Bush™
Volume 2

PRESIDENTIAL SPEAK

"I will have a Vice President who can become the President… I will have a Vice President that agrees with my policy. I'm going to have a Vice President that likes me."

January 2000 Republican presidential debate, Michigan.

★ ★ ★ ★

"We want to develop defenses that are capable of defending ourselves and defenses capable of defending others."

March 29, 2001 Speaking in Washington, D.C.

★ ★ ★ ★

PRESIDENTIALSPEAK

"The war on terror involves Saddam Hussein because of the nature of Saddam Hussein, the history of Saddam Hussein, and his willingness to terrorize himself."

January 29, 2003   Grand Rapids, Michigan.

★ ★ ★ ★

"Let me tell you my thoughts about tax relief. When your economy is kind of oochin' along, it's important to let people have more of their own money."

October 4, 2002   Comments from a speech in Boston, Massachusetts.

★ ★ ★ ★

"Tommy [Thompson] is a good listener, and he's a pretty good actor too."

August 13, 2002 It appears that the President is confusing Secretary of the Department of Health and Human Services Tommy Thompson with United States Senator (and professional actor) Fred Thompson. Waco, Texas.

★ ★ ★ ★

"It's negative to think about blowing each other up. That's not a positive thought."

June 25, 2001 From an interview with *The Wall Street Journal.*

★ ★ ★ ★

"And as I said in my State of the Union, the idea is to see that a car born today—I mean, a child born today—will be driving a car... powered by hydrogen."

February 6, 2003 Speaking on energy independence at the National Building Museum in Washington, D.C.

PRESIDENTIAL SPEAK

"The White House is in Washington, D.C. It's up East."

August 23, 2001 Speaking with students at Crawford Elementary School—"up South" in Crawford, Texas.

★ ★ ★ ★

"My trip to Asia begins here in Japan for an important reason. It begins here because for a century-and-a-half now, America and Japan have formed one of the great and enduring alliances of modern times. From that alliance has come an era of peace in the Pacific."

February 18, 2002 A century-and-a-half of peace, interrupted by World War II. Speaking in Tokyo.

★ ★ ★ ★

The Very Curious Language of George W. Bush™
Volume 2

PRESIDENTIAL SPEAK

"I was proud the other day when both Republicans and Democrats stood with me in the Rose Garden to announce their support for a clear statement of purpose—you disarm or we will."

October 5, 2002   Referring to Saddam Hussein's Iraqi regime in a speech in Manchester, New Hampshire.

"And we'll prevail, because we're a fabulous nation, and we're a fabulous nation because we're a nation full of fabulous people."

January 31, 2002   Speaking in Atlanta, Georgia.

The Very Curious Language of George W. Bush™
Volume 2

PRESIDENTIAL SPEAK

"I understand that the unrest in the Middle East creates unrest throughout the region."

March 13, 2002 Washington, D.C.

★ ★ ★ ★

"We hold dear what our Declaration of Independence says, that all have got uninalienable rights, endowed by a Creator."

May 24, 2002 Moscow, Russia.

★ ★ ★ ★

"In other words, I don't think people ought to be compelled to make the decision which they think is best for their family."

December 11, 2002 Referring to smallpox vaccinations. Washington, D.C.

PRESIDENTIAL SPEAK

"People say: 'How can I help on this war against terror? How can I fight evil?' You can do so by mentoring a child, by going into a shut-in's house and say 'I love you.' "

September 19, 2002 Speaking in Washington, D.C.

"My administration has been calling upon all the leaders in the—in the Middle East to do everything they can to stop the violence, to tell the different parties involved that peace will never happen."

August 13, 2001 Speaking at his ranch in Crawford, Texas.

PRESIDENTIAL SPEAK

"Americans have reached a great consensus about the protection on the environment."

April 22, 2002   Speaking on Earth Day at the Whiteface Mountain Lodge in Wilmington, New York.

"But all in all, it's been a fabulous year for Laura and me."

December 21, 2001   Summing up the year, a little more than three months after September the 11th.

"The United States and Russia are in the midst of a transformationed relationship that will yield peace and progress."

November 13, 2001   Joint press conference at the White House with Russian President Vladimir Putin.

PRESIDENTIAL SPEAK

"These terrorist acts and, you know, the responses have got to end in order for us to get the framework—the groundwork, not the framework—the groundwork to discuss a framework for peace, to lay the—all right."

August 13, 2001   Making reference to former U.S. Senator George Mitchell's Middle East blueprint for peace. Crawford, Texas.

"The reason I believe in a large tax cut because it's what I believe."

December 18, 2000   Washington, D.C.

"I appreciate your sacrifice. I know it's hard to leave a districk that you love... and I want you to know that, um, I feel that you're just as important part of your spouse's mission."

February 9, 2003   Referring to the spouses of members of Congress. Speaking at a Congressional retreat at White Sulphur Springs, West Virginia.

"I appreciate Thomas Downs, who's your superintendent. Interestingly enough, he showed me a picture of he and my dad when he was, I think, a teacher, he said, in Iowa."

May 8, 2002   Speaking at Logan High School in LaCrosse, Wisconsin.

PRESIDENTIAL SPEAK

"And in terms of success of Russia ascending into WTO, it's something that we want."

May 24, 2002 President Bush is referring to the possible 'accession' of Russia into the WTO (World Trade Organization). Meeting with Russian President Vladimir Putin at the Kremlin in Moscow.

"It would be a mistake for the United States Senate to allow any kind of human cloning to come out of that chamber."

April 10, 2002 Washington, D.C.

"We must continue to prosecute corporate criminals… removing executives who break the faith with the shareholders of the American people."

December 10, 2002 Naming William Donaldson to head the Securities and Exchange Commission.

The Very Curious Language of George W. Bush™
Volume 2

PRESIDENTIAL SPEAK

"It's an interesting question about leadership. Does a leader lead, or does a leader follow? Does a leader lead opinion, or does a leader try to chase public opinion? My view is a leader leads."

May 25, 2002   Press conference at St. Petersburg University in Russia.

"Over the long term, the most effective way to conserve energy is by using energy more efficiently."

May 12, 2001   President's weekly radio address.

PRESIDENTIAL SPEAK

Bush: "Let's see, here's my office."

Interviewer: "Oh, nice."

Bush: "Yeah, isn't that neat? And so here's—here's like a stack of reading I'll do this afternoon—with a bunch of letters. And, aaah, I've got some phone calls to make, aah, I've got— probably gonna make a, aaaaah— probably call a couple world leaders today."

August 10, 2001   Giving a tour of the office at his Crawford, Texas, home to an ABC News correspondent.

"Brie and cheese."

August 23, 2001   Speculating on what it is that reporters prefer to eat. The President's ranch in Crawford, Texas.

The Very Curious Language of George W. Bush™

Volume 2

PRESIDENTIAL SPEAK

"Sometimes, when I sleep at night, I think of 'Hop on Pop'."

April 2, 2002   Referring to the Dr. Seuss book. Pennsylvania State University.

Bush: "So what state is Wales in?"
Church: "It's a separate country, next to England."
Bush: "Oh, okay."

October 30, 2001   Speaking with Welsh singer, Charlotte Church.

"The thing that's important for me is to remember what's the most important thing."

February 20, 2001   Speaking to schoolchildren at the Moline Elementary School. St. Louis, Missouri.

PRESIDENTIAL SPEAK

"I'd like to go down to South America. There is a complicating factor there. The Mexican presidential election is taking place, and I certainly don't want to get involved in that."

March 19, 2000   Referring to the upcoming presidential election taking place in the North American country of Mexico. Reported in the *Atlanta Journal-Constitution*.

"With all due respect to the cameras, I hope you read more than you watch TV."

May 8, 2002   Speaking at the Clarke Street Elementary School in Milwaukee, Wisconsin.

PRESIDENTIAL SPEAK

"A politician who takes a poll to figure out what to believe is a politician who is constantly going to be trying to lead through—it's like a dog chasing its tail."

May 25, 2002 St. Petersburg University, Russia.

"They hide in caves. See, this is a different kind of war. And part of my responsibilities as your President is to remind people about the realities that we face in America. One of the realities is, is that these people hide in caves."

September 5, 2002 Speaking in South Bend, Indiana.

PRESIDENTIAL SPEAK

"I want to remind your kids that when it came to enforcing the doctrine that said either—the doctrine said, if you harbor one of those killers, you're just as guilty as the killers—that we went into Afghanistan—the first theater we went into—as a great country, with friends, but we went in not to conquer anybody, not to conquer anybody."

September 23, 2002   Trenton, New Jersey.

★ ★ ★ ★

"We'll be a country where the fabrics are made up of groups and loving centers."

March 27, 2001   Speaking at Western Michigan University in Kalamazoo.

★ ★ ★ ★

The Very Curious Language of George W. Bush™
Volume 2

"Our economy is kind of bumpin' along. It's not as strong as it should be. It's bumpin' and bumpin'."

November 4, 2002 Addressing an audience in Cedar Rapids, Iowa.

"The people who care more about that land are the hard-working farmers and ranchers of your part of the state of Washington, D.C."

September, 2000 Speaking in Spokane, Washington.

"I am here to make an announcement that this Thursday ticket counters and airplanes will fly out of Ronald Reagan Airport."

October 3, 2001   Announcing the re-opening of Ronald Reagan Airport three weeks after the September 11th terrorist attacks. Speaking in Washington, D.C.

"America, at one time, was protected by two oceans. We seemed totally invulnerable to, for example, the wars that took place here in Russia or on the European continent."

May 24, 2002   Speaking in Moscow, Russia, located on the Continent of Europe (900 miles west of Europe's eastern boundary).

PRESIDENTIALSPEAK

"[He] is a man who invaded two countries twice—two countries, once each time."

September 25, 2002 Referring to the Iraqi leader, Saddam Hussein. Speaking in Washington, D.C.

★ ★ ★ ★

"I'm honored that Governor Shaheen is here today. I appreciate her taking time out of her schedule to come and pay her respects to the Presidency."

October 5, 2002 Manchester, New Hampshire.

★ ★ ★ ★

"I have said that the sanction regime is like Swiss cheese. That meant that they weren't very effective."

February 22, 2001 Speaking in Washington, D.C.

PRESIDENTIAL SPEAK

"Oftentimes what I try to say in Washington gets filtered and sometimes my words in Washington don't exactly translate directly to the people."

March 27, 2001 Speaking in Kalamazoo, Michigan.

"How much time do we need to see clearly that he's not disarming? As I said, this looks like a re-run of a bad movie and I'm not interested in watchin' it."

January 21, 2003 Referring to the demand on Iraq to disarm. Speaking to reporters at the White House.

The Very Curious Language of George W. Bush™
Volume 2

"We have just passed historic reform in Washington, D.C.—education reform. It may be hard for you to believe, but there are, at moments, when Republicans and Democrats come together for the good of the nation."

May 10, 2002 Speaking in Columbus, Ohio, at a political luncheon.

"If you believe every child can learn, therefore we ought to know whether that's the case."

August 7, 2002 Speaking at a political function in Jackson, Mississippi.

PRESIDENTIAL SPEAK

"I want to thank you for taking time out of your day to come and witness my hanging."

January 4, 2002 Speaking in Austin, Texas, at a ceremony celebrating the unveiling of his portrait.

"I must confess, it did confuse some of the folks at the Crawford, Texas, coffee shop when I was traveling around the country with Theodore Kennedy."

May 13, 2002 The President is referring to United States Senator Edward Kennedy. Chicago, Illinois.

"It's the systems that don't test are those that quit on the kids."

September 4, 2002 Speaking from the White House about education reform. Washington, D.C.

PRESIDENTIAL SPEAK

"[They] kind of ooch around the dark corners of the world and look out—peep out—around the corner."

October 22, 2002   Referring to terrorists. Downingtown, Pennsylvania.

"You'll hear we're going to spend—the government is going to spend the government money here and the government is going to spend the government here."

September 23, 2002   Trenton, New Jersey.

"My most important job is to defend the homeland—to protect innocent Americans from the deaths of the killers."

June 19, 2002   Washington, D.C.

The Very Curious Language of George W. Bush™
Volume 2

PRESIDENTIAL SPEAK

"Now here she is, the First Lady of the United States. Thank goodness. What a fabulous job she is doing... And Fred Thompson is leading that charge. And as he succeeds, and when he succeeds, he will leave behind a fabulous legacy for future administrations and Senators... [Lamar Alexander] loves his family, he loves his country, he's got fabulous values... I named a fabulous woman out of Texas, named Priscilla Owen, to the 5th Court."

September 17, 2002   Nashville, Tennessee.

★ ★ ★ ★

"We've got to make sure that the education system throughout the world provides people the need to be able to provide work."

December 4, 2001 Speaking to Barbara Walters of ABC News.

"If you put your mind to it, the first-time home buyer, the low-income home buyer, can have just as nice a house as anybody else."

October 15, 2002 Speaking in Washington, D.C.

PRESIDENTIAL SPEAK

"The other day, as you noticed, there was a fellow hiding in the dark caves—or dark corners, not caves. It was in the city—dark, dark corners of a city in Pakistan."

September 23, 2002   Referring to a suspected terrorist arrested by authorities in Pakistan. Speaking in Trenton, New Jersey.

"I remember telling people that where I came from, at least the economic book that I believe in, say if you've got tough times in your economy you got to let people keep more of their own money."

August 22, 2002   Speaking in Central Point, Oregon

PRESIDENTIAL SPEAK

"Speaking about barbaric regimes, we must deal with probably one of the most—not probably—one of the most real threats we face, and that is the idea of a barbaric regime teaming up with a terrorist network and providing weapons of mass destruction—to hold the United States and our allies and our friends blackmail."

September 17, 2002   Nashville, Tennessee.

"I understand how tender the free enterprise system can be."

July 9, 2002   Speaking to the press in the White House. Washington, D.C.

PRESIDENTIAL SPEAK

"I've got a preference for friends."

February 5, 2001 Speaking to the press after meeting with Canadian Prime Minister Jean Chretien. Washington, D.C.

"So today I ask you to challenge your listeners to love somebody just like they'd like to be loved themselves—to remind them that one person can make a difference in somebody's life, to encourage them to mentor, to encourage them to start a ministry which will find the children of those who are incarsinated and love them."

February 10, 2003 Nashville, Tennessee.

The Very Curious Language of George W. Bush™
Volume 2

"I've been to war. I've raised twins. If I had a choice, I'd rather go to war."

January 27, 2002

★ ★ ★ ★

"My pro-life position is I believe there's life. It's not necessarily based in religion. I think there's a life there; therefore, the notion of life, liberty, and pursuit of happiness."

January 23, 2001   As quoted in the *San Francisco Chronicle*.

★ ★ ★ ★

"I met a young lady, a junior in college… I want to thank her for her mentorship."

January 30, 2003   Boys and Girls Club of Greater Washington, D.C.

PRESIDENTIAL✺SPEAK

"Maybe she'll be able to join us in Florida. If not, she can clean out her room."

December 26, 2000 Referring to one of his daughters.

"I believe that one of these days we're going to have brand new types of cars that are going to make us less dependent on foreign sources of crude oil, and we'll be more better at cleaning our air."

April 15, 2002 Cedar Rapids, Iowa.

PRESIDENTIAL SPEAK

"There's an old saying in Tennessee—
I know it's in Texas, probably in
Tennessee—that says 'fool me once,
shame on—shame on you. You fool
me—can't get fooled again.'"

September 17, 2002 Speaking in Nashville, Tennessee.

"I'm confident we can work with
Congress to come up with an
economic stimulus package that will
send a clear signal to the risk-takers
and capital formators of our country."

September 17, 2001 Speaking in Washington, D.C.

The Very Curious Language of George W. Bush™
Volume 2

PRESIDENTIAL SPEAK

"But if you've been laid off of work, you're 100% unemployed."

September 3, 2001   Green Bay, Wisconsin.

★ ★ ★ ★

"[The Prime Minister] talked about non-performing loans, the devaluation issue and regulatory reform. And he placed equal emphasis on all three."

February 18, 2002   Speaking to the press in Tokyo after meeting with Japanese Prime Minister Junichiro Koizumi. The President's staff later made clear that Mr. Bush had meant to say the "deflation" issue, not the "devaluation" issue—a mispronunciation that may have actually affected the value of the yen, Japan's currency.

★ ★ ★ ★

"There was wars on other continents, but we were safe."

February 10, 2003   Referring to life before September 11, 2001.

The Very Curious Language of George W. Bush™
Volume 2

"I want to thank the dozens of welfare-to-work stories, the actual examples of people who made the firm and solemn commitment to work hard to embetter themselves."

April 18, 2002 Washington, D.C.

"I think it's very important for world leaders to understand that, when a new administration comes in, the new administration will be running the foreign policy."

January 12, 2001 Quoted in *USA Today.*

PRESIDENTIAL✺SPEAK

"We're going to stay in Afghanistan to hunt down the killers. They still lurk around. They occasionally come in and we'll find 'em. They kind of bunch up somewhere…"

September 26, 2002   Houston, Texas.

"An ownership society is a compassionate society."

October 15, 2002   Washington, D.C.

"Some of the greatest programs—initiatives—come out of our faith-based programs, or faith-based churches or synagogues or mosques."

January 30, 2003   Speaking in Washington, D.C.

The Very Curious Language of George W. Bush™
Volume 2

PRESIDENTIAL SPEAK

"There is no such thing as legacies. At least there is a legacy, but I'll never see it."

January 31, 2001   Speaking at the White House. Washington, D.C.

"I want to thank your Governor for traveling with me today. It's an honor to be in a presence who has made public education his top priority."

May 8, 2002   Speaking in Milwaukee, Wisconsin, at the Rufus King High School.

"The best way to battle an economic slowdown is to get people your own money back so you can spend it."

March 1, 2002   Speaking to an audience in Des Molnes, Iowa.

The Very Curious Language of George W. Bush™
Volume 2

"It's a commission not only to convince our fellow citizens to love one another just like we like to be loved. It's a commission also to devise practical ways to encourage others to serve. And one practical way is for the development of an award that Americans from all walks of life all around our country will be able to post boldly on their wall, that says, 'I served this great country by loving somebody.' "

January 30, 2003   Washington, D.C.

PRESIDENTIAL SPEAK

"Russia's most precious resource is the brain power of this country. And you've got a lot of it. It's going to take a lot of brains in Russia to create a drain."

May 25, 2002   Answering a question about 'brain drain' at St. Petersburg University in St. Petersburg, Russia.

Reporter: "I want to ask what your message is to the Iraqi people?"
Bush: "You're free, and freedom is beautiful and, aah, you know, it'll take time to restore chaos and order..."

April 13, 2003   Speaking to reporters on the White House lawn. Washington, D.C.

PRESIDENTIAL SPEAK

"In the way they're kind of writing it right now out of the Senate Finance Committee, some people could spend their entire five years on welfare—there's a five year work requirement—going to college. Now that's not my view of helping people become independent, and it's certainly not my view of understanding the importance of work and helping people achieve the dignity necessary so they can live a free life, free from government control."

July 29, 2002   Speaking before a student audience at West Ashley High School in Charleston, South Carolina.

PRESIDENTIAL SPEAK

"There's nothing more deep than recognizing Israel's right to exist. That's the most deep thought of all… I can't think of anything more deep than that right."

March 13, 2002 Washington, D.C.

"Imagine how less dependent America will be on foreign sources of energy and how more easy it'll be to clean up our air."

February 25, 2002 Washington, D.C.

"I admit it. I am not one of the great linguists."

January 23, 2001 Speaking with Tom Brokaw of NBC News. White House, Washington, D.C.

2004 Desk Calendar of Presidential (Mis)Speak

Completely Updated
★ All New Quotes ★

Available wherever books and calendars are sold
and at
www.bushcalendar.com

Outland Books
Skaneateles, New York